I0414928

This Book Belongs To:

BY

Home Planners And Journals

This book is copyright protected. Reproducing this book is prohibited and not allowed without the permission of the author. All rights reserved.

www.ingramcontent.com/pod-product-compliance
Lightning Source LLC
Chambersburg PA
CBHW072051280526
45788CB00006B/2257
9781090217202